BRESSINGHAM - A 50 YEAR HISTORY

Alan Herbert Vauser Bloom, born in 1906, lived with his parents until he was almost 16, in Over, Cambridgeshire. His father, a reluctant general store shopkeeper was much more at ease with his fruit and vegetable growing sideline, a passion that Alan was keen to take up after toying with being a geologist, archaeologist, politician and briefly a bishop.

The family moved to Oakington, to a six-acre small holding, and at 24 in 1931, when Alan's parents moved away, Alan finally had his own business along with a £50 overdraft. During WWII Alan farmed land at Burwell, but by 1945 he was looking to move east.

Alan fell in love with Bressingham: a 'gentleman's small estate and sportsman's paradise with 220 acres'. The asking price was £11,000, and by October 1946 Alan Bloom and family arrived. Two years of hard work followed, but feeling the need for more, on his 41st birthday, Alan saw an advert offering hope of a new life in Canada. A manager was appointed at Bressingham and in September 1948 Alan and family boarded the 'Aquitania' for Canada and then train to Vancouver. The period in Canada was not a success and after rumours were confirmed by the bank manager that 'unless something was done there would be nothing at Bressingham to return to', Alan returned on March 9th 1950.

Although feeling chastened and humbled by his experiences, Alan now felt that although the task ahead at Bressingham was formidable he felt his role was clear cut in the recovery process. Through much hard work in the next few years the Nursery business evolved and surpassed what it had been before. In 1953 Alan dug the first 'Island Beds', but it took until 1957 before work began properly

on the Dell Garde~ ~~~~~~~~~~ Bressingham Ga~~~~~~~~~~ Sunday a month ~~~~~~~~~~

Always looking to ~~~~~~~~~~ 1912 Traction Engine 'Bella', cut up for s~~~~~~~~~~ Canada, Alan bought 'Bertha~~ March 1961, paid for in part from his writing efforts and so his steam collection at Bressingham began. Other traction engines came thick and fast into the collection followed by a 'Foden' steam lorry. Narrow gauge steam locomotives started arriving in 1964 and two years later a passenger service using 'George Sholto' among others commenced. This loco will again be steaming at Bressingham 50 years since Alan brought the first traction engine into the collection.

Following a trip on the 'Flying Scotsman' in 1967 Alan began to think and plan for bigger steam locomotives. 'William Francis' came first in 1968, followed by 'Oliver Cromwell' and then a few years later 'Royal Scot' and the 'Butlins' engines. The centrepiece of Bressingham are the 'Gallopers', which arrived in 1968 and were run by his wife Flora. They have been giving pleasure ever since.

Over the years the narrow gauge railways have been added to and routes changed; there are now three to ride on of differing gauges. Bressingham in this time has gone from opening once a week in the summer, to 50 days a year, now daily between Easter and October. It has become the place for family fun that Alan always intended.

Alan Bloom

WELCOME

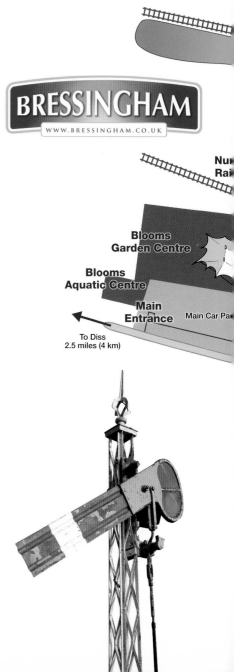

Welcome to Bressingham, a unique day out for all the family. Created from two men's passion for plants, the unrivalled gardens at Bressingham are renowned worldwide for their horticultural excellence. Privately owned by the Bloom family, Adrian Bloom and his father Alan each created a 6-acre (2.4 ha) garden, the Dell and Foggy Bottom. Together with the other linking gardens, there are now over 8,000 species and varieties on display. Alan Bloom's other passion - for steam - led to Bressingham becoming home to a fine collection of traction engines and locomotives. Visitors can ride through the glorious gardens on one of the four working railways or step back in time on the working Victorian steam carousel. With a special-events programme running throughout the summer, there is always something for all the family at Bressingham.

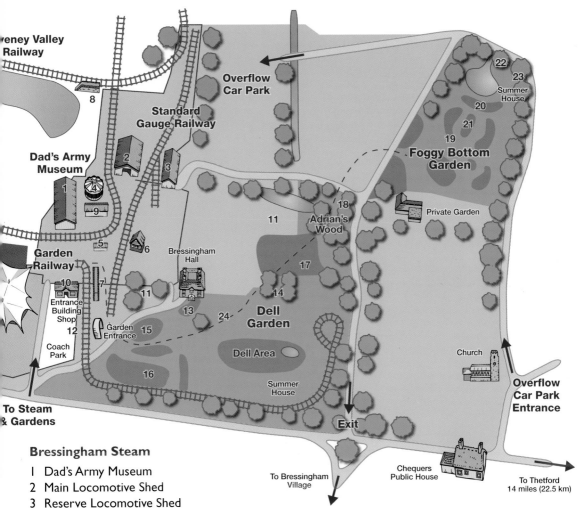

Bressingham Steam

1 Dad's Army Museum
2 Main Locomotive Shed
3 Reserve Locomotive Shed
4 Victorian Gallopers Roundabout
5 Nursery Railway Station
6 Signal Box
7 Garden Railway Turntable and Station
8 Waveney Valley Railway Station
9 Cafe
10 Gift Shop
11 Picnic Areas
12 Pedestrian Crossing to Gardens

Bressingham Gardens

13 Original Island Beds
14 Dell Garden
15 Summer Garden
16 Winter Garden
17 Fragrant Garden
18 Adrian's Wood

19 Foggy Bottom Garden
20 Snake Bed
21 All Seasons Bed
22 Woodland Glade
23 Matt's Summer House
24 Foggy Bottom Trail

3

BRESSINGHAM STEAM

In 1961 Alan Bloom felt a yearning to replace the steam traction engine he had bought for £50 in 1947. It had been used for clearing scrub and sawing wood. With a deep-seated fascination for steam power, Alan was furious on his return from Canada to find it had been cut up and sold for scrap. Having almost finished garden-making, he needed a replacement – just as if the engine had been a pet.

Thousands of steam engines had already gone for scrap, but rarity and nostalgic value were edging prices up. By 1961 Alan was able to buy a Thetford-built Burrell in good condition for £180 and was so thrilled on its arrival that he lost no time in raising steam.

I suppose I kidded myself that Bertha would satisfy me, but when visitors to the gardens also showed interest in her, this opened up new possibilities. One was the excuse to steam up on open days and give little rides to children on the bunker. Another was to search for more engines – and a year later there were fourteen here in various stages of dereliction!'

Alan Bloom

With two or three willing volunteers, Alan scraped away at rust and grime. Two other helpers with 'steam in the blood' were taken on to cope with mechanical and boiler repairs. The workshop was a converted cattle shed, where they sometimes worked on winter evenings, scraping and painting by lantern light. It was Jack Clements, an aged but agile expert who, with Roger Garnham, brought them back to life. All 14 were resplendent in new but traditional liveries by 1964.

STOP
WHEN RED
LIGHT IS SHOWING

WHISTLE

'No.1 *Alan Bloom*' pulling a 'Garden Line' train.

THE RAILWAYS

A History

In the summer of 1964 a 9½ - inch (24cm) gauge track was laid beside the Garden, with a loop at each end to make a 750 - yard (686 metre) trip. 'The Princess', modelled on the LMS type, 1 ton in weight, was able to take 20 or so passengers - it became an immediate success. Subsequently, Alan's trip to the North Wales slate quarries resulted in the arrival of a two - foot (0.6 metre) gauge locomotive, some workmen's seated trucks and a lorry-load of railway track. This was laid in 1965 on a half-mile (800m) route over part of the nursery, one stretch of it being beside the little lake. This was such a success that a much larger track was laid. This became the Nursery Railway.

Nursery Line

The two and half mile - (4km) long track of the Nursery Railway leaves from near the Museum building and passes the locomotive sheds and the lake before crossing over the Waveney Valley Line, where passengers get their first sight of the 15-inch - (38cm) gauge engines waiting to begin their journey from the Lakeside Station.

Turning eastwards, flanked by woods and dykes, the line reaches an area with birch and oak trees and again crosses over the 15-inch gauge line. When both railways are operating, passengers will often see the larger-gauge locomotive giving way to the Nursery Line (below).

There are views of Roydon church and the wilder expanse of Wortham Ling to the south. On the return leg, visitors get an excellent view of the intensive side of the nurseries. In 2010 Bressingham's Engineers under Philip Gray - here since 1971 - built a new locomotive 'Bevan' for the Nursery Railway from parts donated.

One of the two 15-inch (38cm) gauge Krupp, German locomotives operating on the Waveney Valley Railway.

Waveney Valley Railway

Trains on the Waveney Valley Railway leave the Lakeside Station and, travelling east, stop to allow Nursery Line trains to pass before turning south over the Bressingham Drain and running out over low-lying watermeadows. Turning west along the infant River Waveney and the Norfolk-Suffolk county boundary, the line runs through banks of mature rhododendrons to turn north and recross the Bressingham Drain. Here the Waveney Valley Line runs alongside the standard-gauge track.

Garden Railway

The Garden Railway operates from the Dell Garden and the coach park. Its track, alongside the garden, has been lengthened to 1,350 yards (1,234m) and now has a gauge of 10¼ inches (26cm). Designed and built by Bressingham's own engineering team, the line's new locomotive was named Alan Bloom in 1995 and pulls up to sixty people in three carriages. This locomotive is the first to have been built from scratch at Bressingham. With modifications to suit the needs of the Garden Railway, it was modelled on the Hunslet Engine Company's Quarry design.

Standard-Gauge Railway

The Standard-Gauge Line began when David Ward, a British Rail official, told Alan Bloom that several locomotives were languishing for the lack of a good home. The result was the erection of a large building of 13,000 square feet (1,208 sq m) and the provision of ballast and track. This was all completed early in 1968, with generous help for the track work from BR through David Ward. The first big engine to arrive was a unique Garratt articulated locomotive, 'William Francis', from the Coal Board. It was in a deplorable condition and, long before it was restored, two of the allocated BR locomotives arrived. By then Bressingham already had five full-sized locomotives, and more, much smaller standard-gauge engines were acquired. All this was exciting but not satisfactory, because there was only 100 yards (91m) or so of track on which to run them. A longer track could only go south, and the one possible route was the raised, tree-lined causeway. Once the half mile (800m) of line was laid, footplate rides on Oliver Cromwell and the '2500' began, which unfortunately had to end later due to safety regulations.

Waveney Valley Railway

Nursery Railway

GARDEN CENTRE

MAIN CAR PARK

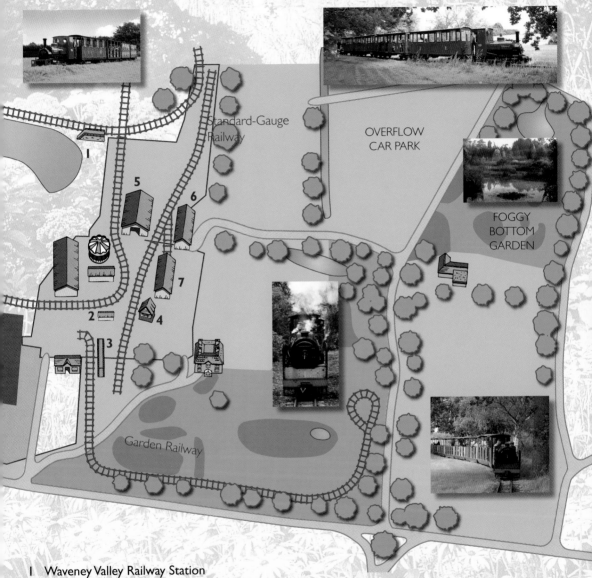

Standard-Gauge Railway

OVERFLOW CAR PARK

FOGGY BOTTOM GARDEN

Garden Railway

1
5
6
7
2
4
3

1 Waveney Valley Railway Station
2 Nursery Railway Station
3 Garden Railway Turntable and Station
4 Signal Box
5 Main Locomotive Shed
6 Reserve Locomotive Shed
7 Locomotive Workshop

Nursery Line	1.31 miles	2.11km	2,310 yards
Garden Line	0.27 miles	0.43km	480 yards
Waveney Line	1.41 miles	2.27km	2,486 yards
Standard Gauge	0.35 miles	0.56km	616 yards

VOLUNTEERS AT BRESSINGHAM

A volunteer drives a Waveney Line train full of summer passengers. Most of the Drivers and Guards you see at Bressingham are volunteers and have been since the services began in 1964.

We are always looking for more... It takes a small army of dedicated staff and volunteers to carry out all the tasks needed to keep the Museum and Gardens in operation.

A Waveney Valley train approaches the diamond crossing to meet the Nursery Line train.

Alan's love of steam has been kept alive by a band of loyal staff and volunteers at Bressingham, who like Alan, are always willing to pass on their knowledge and enthusiasm to a younger generation.

THE LOCOMOTIVES

Throughout Alan Bloom's development of the narrow-gauge railways at Bressingham, he always wished to acquire a standard-gauge steam locomotive. The first exhibit arrived in the main locomotive shed in 1968. Now it contains locomotives of the National Collection.

Two 'Ivatt Atlantic' locomotives of the former
Great Northern Railway, are on loan from the
National Railway Museum.

STANDARD GAUGE PRESERVATION

When the age of steam came to an end and steam locomotives were replaced by diesel, the vast majority of steam engines were cut up for scrap. At that stage there was no heritage railway movement and there was little interest in preserving the locomotives, which is why today, there are relatively few main line steam locomotives still in existence. However, one man who saw a use for the locomotives was (Sir) Billy Butlin. He realised that it has been the dream of every small boy to be an engine driver. He bought a number of locomotives to send to his holiday camps around the country so that former drivers could talk enthusiastically to young 'campers' about life on the railways.

After some 10 years it was decided that the holiday camps needed something new and Butlin's decided to remove the locomotives. This was the opportunity for which Alan Bloom had been waiting

and it was agreed that Royal Scot, Duchess of Sutherland, Granville and Martello should come from their seaside retirement homes to Bressingham on 'permanent loan'. They remained on loan until 1989, when the Rank Organisation, now the owners of Butlins, decided to sell the locomotives and after some difficult negotiations a price was agreed and all 4 locomotives became the property of Bressingham. At first the locomotives were restored and steamed at Bressingham but ever more stringent safety legislation and the escalating cost of boiler work in particular made this impractical. Further, the Trustees realised that the short stretch of main line at Bressingham was not the right location for running main line express locomotives.

OPPOSITE BELOW:
*'The Royal Scot' – one
of the most famous
steam locomotives in
the world. Restored
by Bressingham to full
working order with the
help of a grant from
the Heritage Lottery
Fund. Now in a private
collection.*

'The Duchess of Sutherland' was transferred to the Princess Royal Trust for restoration. With the support of the Heritage Lottery Fund it was decided to try and restore 'No 6100, Royal Scot', but in the end it was clear that there was too much work needed for Bressingham to be able to complete the project and this locomotive had now been transferred to the Royal Scot and General Trust where the restoration is being completed and the locomotive will appear on the main line at some stage in 2011.

'Martello' has been restored in-house at Bressingham and is very much a work-horse on our standard gauge demonstration track and 'Granville' is on display in the main locomotive shed.

BELOW: 'Great Eastern Railway E4 Class No. 490' was designed for cross-country excursion and slow main-line duties in East Anglia. It spent many years working the Cambridge-Mildenhall branch. The E4 is on loan from the National Railway Museum.

'Martello' - former London, Brighton & South Coast Railway No.662, now restored and operational at Bressingham.

'Granville' - former London & South Western Railway Class B4 which was rescued from Southampton Docks, where it acted as a shunting locomotive.

No. 662 'Martello' operational on the Standard Gauge Line.

Great Northern Railway No.990 'Henry Oakley' at Bressingham. On loan from the National Railway Museum.

DIEU ET MON DROIT

THE ROYAL COACHES

Bressingham is home to two Royal Coaches. Queen Alexandra's Saloon is the older and most ornate. Introduced in 1908 and built for the East Coast Joint Stock Company (carriage 396) it is constructed from Javan pine and veneered inside with woods from Commonwealth countries. Originally designed for King Edward VII and Queen Alexandra it was, in more modern times, often used by HM The Queen and the Duke of Edinburgh. Withdrawn from Royal service in 1979 it has been at Bressingham ever since.

Carriage 2901 - Royal Household carriage is an altogether more modern affair being built in 1957 for use by the current Queen's Private Secretary and Lady in Waiting. When Charles became the Prince of Wales, he used the vehicle frequently.

OPPOSITE:
The arms of HM The Queen
on the side of
'Queen Alexandra's Saloon'.

RAYDON WOOD SIGNAL BOX

The signal box was built at Raydon Wood in 1841 on the branch line leading from the Ipswich – London line to Hadleigh.

The line was very lightly used and closed to passengers in 1932 but remained open for freight until 1965. The signal box became redundant in 1932, dismantled and re-erected in a builder's yard in the village. For some time the box was used for the storage of coffins. It was donated to Bressingham in 1997 where it has since been restored using the equipment previously rescued from Oakington signal box in Cambridgeshire.

A typical lower quadrant signal. Many thousands of these were used to control Britain's railways. Nearly all have been replaced by coloured lights.

Some young visitors having a go at signalling.

OPPOSITE:
Oakington signal box frame restored at Bressingham for the public to use - a piece of railway history close to Alan Bloom's first Nursery that followed him to Bressingham.

TRAIN ON LINE

TRACTION ENGINES

'BERTHA'
FIRST OF THE MANY

Traction engine No. 3112 - built in 1909 just a few miles away in Thetford and later to become 'Bertha' - was the engine responsible for igniting one man's dream for steam engines.

Having been restored by Gerald Dixon from a scrapyard state, No. 3112 was hunted down by Alan Bloom to replace his earlier much missed 'Bella' and purchased in March 1961 for the sum of £180. Rather than satisfying Alan's want for steam at his beloved Bressingham, 'Bertha' fuelled it.

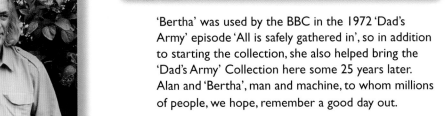

'Bertha' was used by the BBC in the 1972 'Dad's Army' episode 'All is safely gathered in', so in addition to starting the collection, she also helped bring the 'Dad's Army' Collection here some 25 years later. Alan and 'Bertha', man and machine, to whom millions of people, we hope, remember a good day out.

BOXER

PW 1714

Burrell

Built in 1932 - 'Boadicea' is one of the last steam lorries built by Foden.

'Bunty' built by Richard Garrett & Sons in 1924.

A visiting traction engine demonstrating timber cutting.

The traction engines were the first arrivals at Bressingham and make an impressive display in the main exhibition hall. Many of them were built only 14 miles (22.5km) away at the famous Burrell works in Thetford. They include portable engines and road-rollers. 'Bunty' was built by Richard Garrett & Sons of Leiston, Suffolk in 1924 and was exhibited at the Smithfield Show. Later, in 1925, it was sold to Clare District Council for hauling road-mending stone. It is now restored to its special show livery of chocolate brown with red wheels and can be seen operating at Bressingham.

STATIONARY ENGINES

The stationary engines are housed on one side of the main locomotive shed. On entering the building is the massive Easton & Anderson beam-engine, which was originally installed in 1870 to supply water to Banstead Hospital, Surrey. Alongside is a display of industrial engines, including a Sir William Arrol & Company horizontal pumping engine, known as the Chivers 'Jam' engine. Built in Glasgow in 1902, it was used in the Chivers jam factory at Histon, near Cambridge. It provided hydraulic power for lifts that transported trolleys of produce and ingredients within the factory. A boiler provides a steam feed to the fine array of stationary engines at Bressingham, enabling visitors to see these powerful engines at work on steam days.

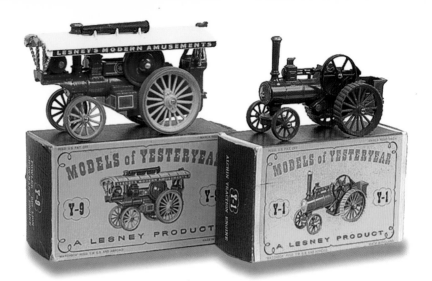

The enduring attraction and excitement of playing with 'Boys Toys' is reflected in these beautiful 1950s die-cast models of traction engines - just like their real counterparts here at Bressingham.

THE GALLOPERS

Bressingham's steam centrepiece is the magnificent three-abreast Gallopers – the horses on the Victorian roundabout. It is one of the finest to be seen anywhere. Built by Savages of King's Lynn in 1900 and owned and operated by the Thurston family of Norfolk until 1934, the Gallopers later opened at Whitley Bay and ended up in Brechin, Fife.

The engine was originally built by Tidmans of Norwich but has been completely rebuilt at Bressingham.

The Gallopers came to Bressingham in 1968 and it was only with hard work over a long period that it reached its present superb condition. During the main season it operates every day giving rides to young and old.

Riding the horses of the famous Gallopers carousel – a favourite for the young and old.

THE DAD'S ARMY

COLLECTION

The BBC television series 'Dad's Army' ran from 1968 to 1977 with a total of 80 episodes broadcast. Today, this legendary comedy series is still shown with regular repeats delighting viewers of all ages. Not only did it make household names of the cast, but it also introduced an ensemble of characters and catchphrases that will live long in the viewer's memory.

Created by David Croft and Jimmy Perry, Dad's Army was often filmed in and around Thetford, with several vehicles from Bressingham making guest appearances over the years.

Today, the fictional town of Walmington-on-Sea is brought to life at Bressingham: walk down the high street and visit Captain Mainwaring's bank, the church hall and Jones's butcher's shop. Re-creating the wartime atmosphere of the show, visitors can see original uniforms and props from this most enduring and loved of British situation comedies.

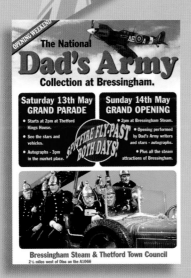

OPPOSITE:
The main characters and writer and producer/director of the famous 'Dad's Army' series.

A reproduction of Walmington-on-Sea, the fictional home of the 'Dad's Army' platoon.

"Let 'em all come"

MEN 41-55

HOME DEFENCE BATTALIONS

Apply at any Army Recruiting Centre Now

Hitler will send no warning – so always carry your gas mask

ISSUED BY THE MINISTRY OF HOME SECURITY

DIG FOR VICTORY

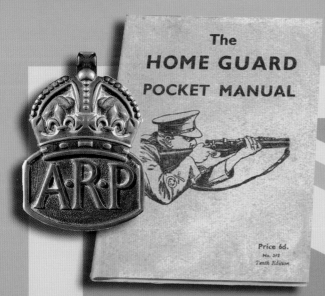

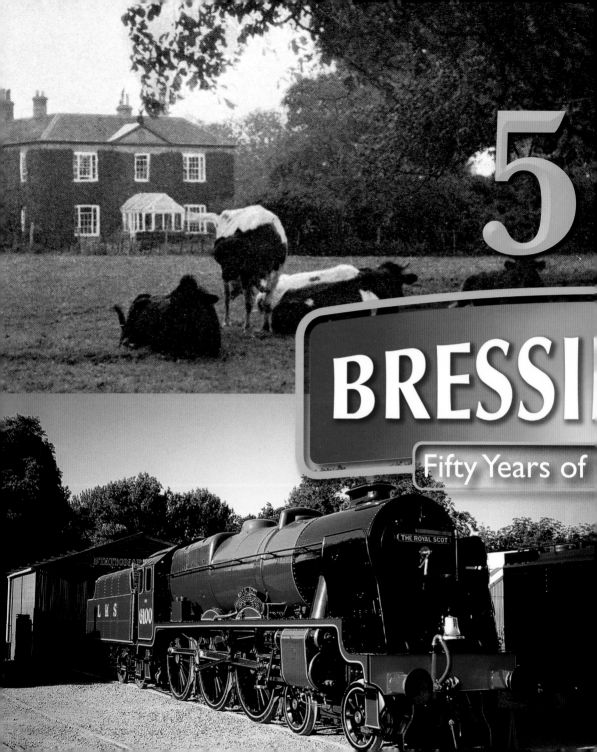

5

BRESSI

Fifty Years of

The Bressingham Gardens

Bressingham has long been acknowledged as a world centre of horticulture through its famous nurseries and gardens, but few gardeners are aware of recent developments that have added greater breadth of interest to attract knowledgeable horticulturists and beginner gardeners alike.

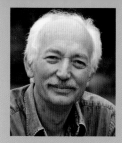

Introduction by Adrian Bloom

Welcome to The Bressingham Gardens. If you have never visited the gardens before, or haven't visited for some time, we hope you will be more than pleasantly surprised. As you will gather from the brief history and introduction to the six distinct areas of gardens on this double-page spread, a lot has been happening. From the heritage of the Dell Garden - created by my father, Alan Bloom, between 1953 and 1962 - and my own garden, Foggy Bottom (started in 1967 and still going!), a unified set of gardens has developed, now mounting to approximately 16 acres (6.ha). The Bloom family inherited a passion for plants from Alan Bloom, who died in 2005, aged 98. We hope that this passion, and the knowledge that comes from it, shows in the gardens and will make your visit - with this brochure as a guide - more interesting and rewarding. If you live locally it would certainly be worthwhile purchasing a season ticket, so that you can see The Bressingham Gardens change from Spring through to Autumn - and then come and see the new Winter Garden too.

Enjoy your visit

The Gardens in brief

The main two world-famous six-acre (2.4ha) gardens are the Dell Garden, created by the late Alan Bloom and Foggy Bottom Garden created by his son Adrian. The four newer gardens which link the two have been designed by Adrian Bloom and planted with the assistance of the expert garden staff at Bressingham. The gardens are described chronologically below.

Alan Bloom's Dell Garden

In 1953, Alan Bloom, founder of the family nursery, which by that time had become one of the largest in the country growing hardy perennials, wanted to experiment with a new way of growing them in island beds. His first beds (looking much the same today) were planted in front of the family home, Bressingham Hall, and - proving successful - were soon being planted in adjacent meadows, eventually numbering 48 beds and covering six acres (2.4ha). Alan, a renowned perennial plantsman, collected plants from all over Europe, ending up by 1962 with nearly 5,000 different species and varieties, making this an important as well as a beautiful historical collection. This garden, now looked after by Alan's son-in-law, Curator Jaime Blake, will amaze you with its rolling open landscape, its colour and variety - truly a Mecca for perennial-lovers.

Adrian Bloom's Foggy Bottom Garden

Adrian joined the family business in 1962 and soon became keen to create his own garden, wanting to experiment with planting for year-round colour using primarily conifers and heathers. His first plantings in 1966 were on the site of an empty meadow and a new house in one corner. With his wife Rosemary, he was able to gradually develop a six acre (2.4ha) garden which he called Foggy Bottom. Over 500 different conifers and 100 heathers created an impact across the country, so popular did they become. Now a wealth of mature conifers, trees and shrubs from all over the world, add a backdrop to ornamental grasses and perennials. This garden continues to develop and change so there is always something new for visitors to see.

The Summer Garden

This garden was created in 2001 from an old meadow as part of a new, more pleasing entrance to the Dell Garden. It was planted primarily with many varieties of *Miscanthus sinensis*, a Japanese ornamental grass. In late summer these grasses, which grow from 3ft (90cm) or less to 10ft (3m) in one season, are spectacular as a backdrop to colourful summer-flowering perennials which drift among them, including a spectacular 'river' of Geranium 'Rozanne', and other innovative plantings.

Adrian's Wood
In 2001 a new pathway was built connecting the Dell Garden with Foggy Bottom, cutting out the long trip through the Steam Museum, which for the previous 30 years had been used by visitors to Foggy Bottom. This area, originally planted by Adrian Bloom in 1964 - 65 with trees and conifers, including five giant redwoods, *Sequoiadendron giganteum*, had become overgrown and almost impenetrable. Now, after felling many trees, including 30, 60ft - (18m) high Leyland cypress, Adrian is replanting with entirely North American-origin plants - now a place to stop and enjoy the spectacle as well as to pass through to Foggy Bottom.

The Winter Garden
Close to the entrance of the Garden Centre and Steam Museum, this garden opened in November 2006, and planted specifically with plants of winter interest. On a winter's day and even into spring, the spectacle of coloured stems of *Cornus* 'Midwinter Fire', flowers of snowdrops, early bulbs, hellebores and winter-flowering heathers will lift your spirits and hopefully encourage you to consider planting your own winter-interest garden.

The Fragrant Garden
From the first conifer and heather beds planted by Adrian Bloom in 1963, then in 1980 replanted as a shrub garden, another new, remodelled garden is emerging. This is being designed and planted with an interesting range of plants with fragrant flowers and foliage. It is situated next to the picnic area, where visitors can enjoy flowers and fragrance throughout the summer.

Even in winter the garden has colour and interest. The beautiful blooms of Mollis X Intermedia Pallida, covered by snow in early February.

The Bressingham Gardens Tour

Follow our guide through the gardens on the Foggy Bottom Trail, enjoying the Summer Garden (passing by or meandering through the Winter Garden), Alan Bloom's Dell Garden, the Fragrant Garden, Adrian's Wood and finally to Foggy Bottom, Adrian and Rosemary Bloom's private garden.

The Entrance and Summer Garden

Three small island beds surround the arch which bears the description 'Welcome to Bressingham Gardens'. Check the Gardens sign as you cross the Bressingham Hall driveway and ahead of you is the Summer Garden, whose main interest starts in May. The large beds, planted in 2001 by Adrian Bloom, Jaime Blake and the garden staff, are dissected by curving grass pathways. To your right is the Winter Garden, which, though attractive in summer, is primarily of interest from November through to April.

The Summer Garden houses part of the National Collection of *Miscanthus*, a wonderful range of ornamental grasses which literally form the 'backbone' to this garden. The taller varieties emerge from ground level in spring to reach from 8 -10ft (2-3m) by August, massed with crimson or silvery plumes which wave in the wind. Some are much shorter and suitable for smaller gardens, and many have variegated leaves which give a longer period of interest.

As they start to die back in autumn, the foliage and plumes continue to remain attractive through winter. Even with this collection, *miscanthus* on their own might look boring, but as you'll certainly notice, colourful summer perennials meandering amongst them make for vivid viewing. A striking blue river of Geranium 'Rozanne', which flowers from June until autumn frosts, is one of the highlights, as are other perennials such as Geranium 'Patricia', many *Agapanthus*, the hardy African lilies, including the Bressingham-raised *Crocosmia* 'Lucifer', 'Vulcan' and 'Spitfire'. Our recommendations from the Summer Garden for your garden are *Miscanthus sinensis* 'Morning Light', 'Ferner Osten' and 'Strictus'.

Some of the plumes of miscanthus are very striking such as this *Miscanthus sinensis* 'Zwergelefant'.

The National Collection of Miscanthus

We are pleased to hold this important collection of Japanese ornamental grasses at Bressingham. This is only one of hundreds of collections of garden plants nationwide under the auspices of Plant Heritage, a registered charity. As a collection holder we aim to keep up-to-date trials of new introductions and maintain established varieties. At present we have over 80 varieties with most being on show in the narrow beds near the picnic area and Adrian's Wood.

The superb hardy 'Geranium Rozanne' forms a river of blue in the Summer Garden, highlighted by the yellow flowers of 'Heliopsis Loraine Sunshine' and other perennials with taller 'Miscanthus' in the background'.

LEFT: Bressingham Hall and meadows in 1950.

MAIN PICTURE: with the original island beds of perennials in front. Why not stay for bed and breakfast in the heart of the gardens?

The Dell Garden

Having perused the Summer Garden by now you will probably have turned to look in the distance at Bressingham Hall, an imposing ivy-clad Georgian mansion, with colourful island beds in front of the Hall where Alan Bloom started his garden back in 1953. We recommend you look first at these beds, which Alan created as an experiment, before entering the main Dell Garden lying between the Hall and the A1066 which runs to the north. Alan Bloom's son-in-law, Jaime Blake, Dell Garden Curator, maintains these plantings in front of the Hall much as they have always been, and many of the plants, such as *Paeonia mlokosewitschii* and *Scabiosa graminifolia*, are, amazingly, still the originals.

Go past the old wooden summerhouse near the sycamore and you will come to a flat meadow with more island beds. In this area is one of the most spectacular plants - at least during its flowering period in June and July. It is not a perennial but a very fine selection of the Japanese dogwood, *Cornus kousa chinensis* which we've called 'Bressingham'. In midsummer its mass of white bracts literally stops visitors in their tracks! If it's not in flower there is plenty else to see here, including an imposing specimen of *Picea morika* 'Pendula', which was planted in 1996 to commemorate Robert Bloom, Adrian's brother, who was tragically killed in a car crash the previous September. Now, heading west away from the Hall, you come to a small bridge, which Alan Bloom built in 1958 out of local Norfolk flints. Alan believed that this low area called 'the Dell' which you are now overlooking, had been created from clay excavated from this area for brick making. In 1958, with meadows still either side, the farm's cows could walk from one to the other, allowing garden visitors to walk beneath into the newly created Dell

Garden. In this beautiful garden are many shade and moisture-loving plants, leading down to the small pond at the other end. Building with flints became another of Alan Bloom's passions, and perhaps his most visible building is the flintstone summerhouse with the thatched roof, beside which is a large weeping willow, *Salix babylonica* 'Pendula'. Above the pond, surrounded by yet another flint wall, is a wonderful view back across the Dell.

There is still perhaps a third of the Dell Garden to see to the south of the Dell: long curved beds with cleverly landscaped undulations to take away the flatness of the original meadow. Here are ornamental grasses and perennials, with one long bed planted with low-growing perennials and alpine plants. The grey brick walls of the back of the Hall can be seen in the distance, to give perspective as you walk towards the grouping of tall Scots pines (*Pinus sylvestris*) and beyond the Fragrant Garden, Adrian's Wood and Foggy Bottom. There are many rare and unusual plants in the Dell Garden and all are clearly labelled, so it's a magnet for those who wish to learn.

Clematis heracleifolia 'Alan Bloom'

A historical perspective -

Alan Bloom's Island Beds

Alan Bloom was first a nurseryman and a perennial plant expert, but it was not until 1953, when he had successfully re-established Blooms Nurseries at Bressingham, that he took time to start gardening with perennials in front of Bressingham Hall. From a vacant lawn he cut and prepared informal beds, each surrounded by grass pathways, his 'islands'. Groups of perennials were selected according to height, form and flowering season, with taller plants in the centre, supported without staking (very prevalent in those days) by shorter varieties around the outside. With more light and air, the perennials grew sturdier, providing a succession of colour and interest, with the main peak between June and September, creating the impact he was looking for. In general gardening terms, this idea was not totally unique, but for perennials alone it was quite revolutionary. Never one to do anything by halves, Alan continued over the next few years to plant nearly six acres (2.4ha) of beds, planted with around 5,000 species and varieties of perennials.

ABOVE: The late Alan Bloom with Dell Garden Curator, Jaime Blake, in 2000 beside Clematis heracleifolia 'Alan Bloom', named after the originator.

The Fragrant Garden

Now follow the signs to Foggy Bottom, which will take you beneath the Scots pine into the still developing Fragrant Garden (which used to be known as the Shrub Garden). As you walk into this area of perhaps half an acre (0.2 ha), you will see relatively small beds to the right and left and an open vista in front of you. The beds were first planted by Adrian Bloom in 1963, a year after he and elder brother Rob joined the family business. These were Adrian's first experimental beds, where he planted dwarf conifers and heathers, prior to planting the Foggy Bottom garden in 1967. In the mid-1980s many more shrubs were planted for visitor interest, and now a third phase is under way, the garden planted with a range of plants with fragrant flowers and foliage, particularly for summer. The plans are to make a 'romantic' garden over two or three years where visitors can linger and enjoy fragrance,

birds, bees and butterflies on their way to Adrian's Wood and Foggy Bottom. There is much to look forward to in this developing garden, as with all six gardens at Bressingham. You may have spotted the sign to Adrian's Wood on the right, and as you walk in that direction, to the left is the broad open expanse of the picnic area, two large oak trees framing the eastern side, while to the south are the curved narrow beds of the *Miscanthus* collection. If you have a season ticket you'll be fascinated to see their progress through the seasons. Follow the narrow path along the Foggy Bottom Trail to the continuing development that is known as Adrian's Wood, on the way to Foggy Bottom.

BELOW: Dianthus, Eryngium, Lavender and roses make a colourful and fragrant association in the Fragrant Garden during the summer months.

Adrian's Wood

A tribute to a North American horticultural heritage

The British climate allows us to grow an amazing range of plants, one reason perhaps why we have long been considered a 'nation of gardeners'. In our historic quest for travel and colonisation we have discovered and brought back to Britain thousands of plant varieties from across the world. One of the prime sources from the 17th century onwards has been the rich and varied flora and woodlands of North America. Even before their discovery by European explorers and plant hunters, an enormous range of plants had been an integral part of the lives of the native Americans for thousands of years, who used them for their edible, medicinal and practical properties. The Europeans brought plants and seeds to Europe to glorify their gardens, selecting and hybridising many new varieties to enhance their displays. When the giant redwoods were discovered in the Californian Sierra mountains in 1853, this monumental tree was quickly named in England after the British military hero Wellington. Even today some people still call the giant redwood, *Sequoiadendron giganteum*, *Wellingtonia*! During the last century gardeners in the USA and Canada have looked to England and Europe for their inspiration, but seldom have we, in Adrian Bloom's opinion, adequately recognised the debt we owe to that continent, its pre-European culture and its wealth of plant resource which has enriched our garden heritage. This garden is only the beginning of an educational process which will eventually chart the origins of the plants displayed, plus give the ethnobotany (the uses which native Americans had for them), and describe their discovery and introduction by plant hunters and breeders.

Autumn or 'fall' colour in
Adrian's Wood in late October.

Adrian's Wood

Adrian's Wood has a history too. In 1963, with the thought that the gardens might be extended in the future, Alan and Adrian Bloom had a pond dug at the bottom of the meadow below the Fragrant Garden. Adrian planted the banks with a range of trees and taller growing conifers in 1964 and 1965, including some young plants of *Sequoiadendron giganteum*, the giant redwoods, which he had brought back as seed from Squaw Valley, California, in 1960. The rapid-growing *Cupressocyparis leylandii*, a tree fast gaining popularity at that time for hedging, was planted as shelter for other trees in the wood. With other business and garden developments taking precedence, this area was largely left to grow unattended for 35 years, as the trees reached for the sky. Foggy Bottom, created from 1967, was by 2000 famous in its own right, and was now open regularly to the public, so it seemed sensible to Adrian to connect all the gardens together. In 2001, after felling many of the Leyland cypresses, a new curving pathway was built linking the Dell Garden with Foggy Bottom. With the 60ft (18m) high Leylandii gone, the five giant redwoods, now beginning to live up to their reputation at 80ft (20m) high, were revealed. Fitting perhaps that this should be called Adrian's Wood, and that Adrian, who has had close ties with North America throughout his life, wanted to plant this area with entirely North American-origin plants, both species and cultivars (previous page, 'A tribute to a North American horticultural heritage').

From 2001 Adrian's Wood has gradually been developed with an increasing range of interesting trees, shrubs, perennials, grasses and bulbs; some of

LEFT: Two Californian redwoods planted by Adrian Bloom in 1964, Sequoiadendron giganteum (giant redwood) and Sequoiadendron sempervivens (coast redwood), tower above North American perennials.

the seasonal displays are increasingly spectacular. As you walk through and onto the boardwalk, take time to meander along a circular woodland pathway and enjoy the many fine plants in the garden. In spring you'll see the showy yellow spathes of the American skunk cabbage, *Lysichiton americanum*, followed by woodland bulbs and perennials such as trilliums, phlox and dicentras. Native American rhododendrons are mixed with a 'meadow' of *Camassia quamash*, the American counterpart to the British bluebell. From early summer, with its vivid display of bee balm, *Monarda* 'Gardenview Scarlet', to late summer and autumn when displays of *Rudbeckia fulgida var. deamii*, a showy black-eyed Susan, the tall bold joe-pye weed, *Eupatorium purpureum* 'Gateway', and many violet and blue asters make a colourful show, this is a garden to enjoy. These summer perennials are worthwhile plants for most gardens where there is reasonable space. Still on the Foggy Bottom Trail, only another 230ft (70m) to go, across the small wooden bridge and into the top corner of the 18-acre (7.2ha) Gap meadow. Head past three silver birch lined up towards the entrance... and here is the final destination.

Colour in Adrian's Wood

May: Camassia quamash.

July: Monarda 'Gardenview Scarlet'.

September: Rudbeckia fulgida var. deamii and Eupatorium purpureum 'Gateway'.

BELOW: late summer; Adrian's Wood showing just how colourful North American perennials and shrubs can be at this time of year. Monarda, Rudbeckia and Eupatorium are the main perenials featured.

Foggy Bottom - a garden to inspire

Entering the Foggy Bottom garden by the small green kiosk, you will have little idea of the views that will greet you. Prior to 1966, this was an open and flat meadow, like the one you are leaving, and had no building or tree in it. Now, trees and shrubs are on either side of the vistas in front, adding structure and shelter and a feeling of contours. Walk on 30 yards (27m) and look to your right; you will see that up a slight incline the white bark stems of two paperbark birches, *Betula papyrifera*, whilst to your left is a long vista which goes beyond the split-rail fence. Ahead is another vista, from the eastern gate where you have come in, to the western gate just around the far corner beyond. You will see a mixture of maturing conifers, trees and shrubs as the main and colourful backdrop to perennials and ornamental grasses, all of which provide changes throughout the seasons. Originally, from 1967 when the first plant went in, Adrian only developed the area close to the house, using mostly conifers and heathers. A fence ran from east to west to keep the cows in the meadow out. From 1974, the remainder of the meadow was gradually taken in, with the pond at the lower end being dug out in 1978. Frustratingly, although flooding can occur in winter, it wouldn't hold water in summer and an enormous butyl liner was put in during 1980.

Adrian's plan was to have long, mostly broad meandering pathways between large island beds, in time creating long views and vistas with focal points which changed through the season. The increasing conifer and heather collections acted as Alan Bloom's Dell Garden had for perennials, as an experimental ground for plants sold by the nursery. Adrian travelled the world collecting new plants to trial, eventually introducing many of them to British gardeners. Gradually the garden and its plant collection have broadened and changed, but Foggy Bottom remains a treasure trove of plants, with around 3,000 varieties. As they have grown they have required, as most mature gardens do, thinning, pruning and replanting.

Why the name Foggy Bottom?

Whilst the low-lying area of the garden that Adrian and Rosemary Bloom have created often gets misty or foggy during early summer mornings or winter days, it is named after a place called Foggy Bottom in Washington DC, USA. In 1959 Adrian Bloom was working in a nursery in Maryland and helped deliver plants to garden centres in that area. One was at Foggy Bottom (quite near the Pentagon) in Washington and the name stuck in Adrian's mind. Unusual, perhaps, when East Anglian towns such as Norwich and Ipswich have counterparts in New England, named by early settlers from those areas, to have a place in England (even if it is a garden) given an American place name.

A view in summer across the small pond shows perennials and grasses, with a background of conifers and trees. These were planted just over 30 years ago in what was then a flat treeless meadow.

Foggy Bottom in summer. Planting began from a flat open meadow in 1967. Now trees, shrubs and conifers provide structure and a backdrop to perennials and ornamental grasses.

*Foggy Bottom
during its early
conifer and heather
phase in 1980.*

As you walk left down to the pond, you will notice to your right a woodland pathway which takes you through to the All Seasons Bed, one of the more recent highlights of the garden... Some people miss it, so make sure you don't! In summer, as you walk past the fence you'll see the Snake Bed to your right, which has a central spine of a dozen varieties of *Miscanthus* providing the backdrop to colourful summer perennials. Ahead to your left, is a striking combination of *Crocosmia* 'Lucifer' with *Hydrangea arborescens* 'Annabelle', which can be seen from a 100 or more metres away. The pond is almost hidden to your right as you go to cross the slightly elevated bridge, with an atmospheric view across it to perennials, grasses and taller trees beyond. There is good reason to have raised wooden decking through this damp woodland garden with shade-loving plants either side. Notice the golden-leaved beech *Fagus sylvatica* 'Aurea Pendula' to your left, and nestling between the trees, as though it had been there for ever a solidly built summerhouse. Matt's Summerhouse is the final destination of the Foggy Bottom Trail; it was built in 2001 by Matt Bloom, Adrian and Rosemary's middle son, a timber framer by profession. With oak beams and pegged timbers, this traditionally made building offers shelter, a resting point and wonderful views into the garden. There is still much to see in Foggy Bottom before making the trip back. You can explore each pathway, perhaps understanding that you see a garden in its third phase of transition, with woodland pathways being opened up from densely planted beds; more light and air being introduced from thinning older trees and conifers; new planting and new designs being created each year.

As most of the old heather plantings have been replaced, a new bed, the All Seasons Bed, has been planted to continue this tradition, mixed now not only with selected conifers but also with shrubs and ornamental grasses. In summer and autumn the red river of Japanese blood grass, *Imperata cylindrica* 'Rubra', is a spectacular sight. Adrian has adapted and used conifers imaginatively and believes that many can be used as architectural specimens or living statuary. The weeping Atlas cedar, *Cedrus atlantica* 'Glauca Pendula', is a bit of a mouthful to say, but you can see in the Sad Bed near the All Seasons Bed, how a specimen has been trained along a support, while in the TV Bed, two plants have been trained together over a wooden support to make an arch. Notice too in Foggy Bottom how the colour of foliage, be it evergreen or deciduous, has been used to create dramatic contrasts and background to highlight foreground perennials. The garden continues to be transformed as trees as high as 25m / 80ft. are carefully removed and new plantings made. One area is being planted as an Acer Glade for autumn colour and many 'streams' and 'rivers' are being planted, one of Adrian's innovative ideas becoming a feature and popular with gardeners.

56

SPRING

The final destination of the Bressingham Gardens Tour, and the Foggy Bottom Trail is Matt's summer house, seen here across the pond in spring.

SUMMER

Perennials and grasses provide dramatic colour, Monarda Violet Queen, contrasting with Kniphofia Percy's Pride.

AUTUMN

The All Season's Bed is lit up by the flaming crimson foliage of a river of ornamental grass. Imperata cylindrica Rubra, winding through conifers.

Wildlife at Bressingham

Bees, butterflies and much more are set amongst meadows and woodland which are a haven for wildlife, some of whom are more welcome than others!

With 8,000 different plant species and cultivars offering tremendous diversity throughout the year, including trees, conifers, shrubs, perennials, grasses and bulbs, there is shelter and food for a wide variety of animals, birds, bugs and insects. Roe, and muntjac deer browse on plants, moles disturb the soil, fieldmice gnaw at bark, hare and rabbits nibble and grey squirrels scamper to get the annual crop of walnuts before we do!

Wood pigeons eat the new shoots of perennials emerging in spring, but occasionally they will fall prey to a fox or resident sparrowhawk. We don't have badgers or bears but we do have stoats, weasels and hedgehogs. The bees and butterflies are abundant in spring and summer with beautiful dragonflies darting and hawking amongst them and, if you take a seat, you will be able to study the many different bird species as well as the wonderful views of the gardens.

Wildlife offers a new and bigger dimension to visitors of the gardens for both young and old alike and these pages show some of the fascinating small creatures to be seen here.

Healthy Harvest

Jamie Blake, the Dell Garden Curator, has made use of the rich resource of nectar in the gardens by keeping bees nearby and has a limited production of 'Head Gardener's Honey'. When a good harvest is available pots are for sale at the Hall and Museum Shop.

A Honey Bee gathers pollen from an Astrantia flower.

Dragonfly settled on a Salvia plant.

Comma butterfly on Verbena Bonariensis.

Small Tortoiseshell on Sedum Matrona.

Bumblebee and Salvia X Sylvestrus 'Mainacht'.

Bumblebees sleeping around an Aringium 'Big Blue' flower.

The Winter Garden

We have left this exciting recently developed garden until last because most visitors come to Bressingham from spring to autumn and will initially see it at that time as largely a foliage garden, though Geranium 'Rozannne' in particular provides a ribbon of blue through the heathers, grasses and shrubs. The photograph shows just how spectacular some plants can be in winter, a season most of us seldom consider when planning our gardens. Adrian has designed curving pathways through raised beds planted with low-growing grasses and perennials to create a colourful edging through which snowdrops and other bulbs will appear in late winter and early spring. Large drifts of winter-flowering heathers are in full flower from February to April and contrast with other shrubs, particularly the bold, fiery-twigged dogwood, *Cornus sanguinea* 'Midwinter Fire'. To the right another colourful red-twigged dogwood, *Cornus alba sibirica*, contrasts with white-stemmed birches and *Helleborus x nigercors*. Drifts of the Lenten rose, *Helleborus orientalis*, make an appearance beneath the Japanese cherry, and fragrant and scented plants are mixed amongst other winter-flowering and foliage shrubs. Were you to come in February or March you would see masses of crocus between the 'Welcome to Bressingham' sign and the hall driveway, where over 5,000 are planted. You would also be able to see the stunning vista with four recommended plants for your garden prominent: *Cornus sanguinea* 'Midwinter Fire' above the ruby-red foliage of *Bergenia* 'Bressingham Ruby', and the black-leaved *Ophiopogon planiscapus* 'Nigrescens'. Completing the picture is one of our favourite and recommended snowdrops, the robust large-flowered *Galanthus* 'S. Arnott'. More planting extends beyond the new archways of weeping cedars to give a more Mediterranean feel, with evergreens such as Eucalyptus and Photinias playing a role.

Come to Bressingham and lift your spirits in winter. Adrian has designed this garden for maximum colour and impact - make sure you take a few ideas and perhaps plants home with you for your own winter garden area. Contact 01379 686900 for details.